INDUSTRIAL HISTORY IN PICTURES: BRISTOL

The Floating Harbour, Bristol, in 1837 by Joseph Walter (1783-1856)
City Art Gallery, Bristol

INDUSTRIAL HISTORY IN PICTURES:

Bristol

R. A. BUCHANAN
NEIL COSSONS

DAVID & CHARLES : NEWTON ABBOT

7153 4745 4

'PROSPERITY TO THE CITY OF BRISTOL'

In the hope that its citizens will recognise and
enjoy the industrial heritage of their city

Set in Plantin roman
and printed in Great Britain
by W. J. Holman Limited Dawlish
for David & Charles (Publishers) Limited
South Devon House Newton Abbot Devon

CONTENTS

INTRODUCTION

The story of the growth of Bristol covers a thousand years. There are, indeed, iron-age remains on Clifton Downs and relics of Roman occupation at Sea Mills which show that the importance of the region was recognised long before AD 1000. But it was about this time, in late Anglo-Saxon England, that a permanent settlement first grew up at the junction of the River Frome with the Bristol Avon, at a point where it was possible to construct a bridge over the larger river. On this site, sheltered on the west by a range of limestone hills, but with easy access to the open sea along the Avon, grew 'Brig-stowe', the bridge-town. A castle was built to protect the bridge, and around its walls clustered the markets, churches, and a population devoted increasingly to trade and manufacturing industry. Ships brought to its wharves the produce of Severnside and, venturing further afield, the wines and other commodities of France and the Iberian peninsula.

For several centuries Bristol was the undisputed centre of the industrial, social, and political life of the western and south-western regions of England, being second only to London amongst the cities of the kingdom. Since the eighteenth century, the rapid growth of the newer industrial cities of the Midlands and the North has displaced Bristol from this highly favoured position. At the same time, the exploitation of the mineral resources of South Wales and the development of other cities has caused a diminution of its importance in the West Country. Bristol, however, has not stood still in the past two hundred years. Its industries, although more varied and growing more slowly than those of some of its rivals, have developed steadily. While some industrial processes have disappeared, others have appeared to take their place, so that the wealth of the city and its hinterland has continued to increase.

Today, with a population of half a million, Bristol is still the foremost city of the West Country, commanding the vast and variegated industrial development of Severnside and the main lines of communication with Wales and the West. In and around Bristol a new industrial landscape is being created, blending with the surviving landmarks of earlier phases of industrialisation. It is this shifting landscape, with the new perpetually emerging from amongst the old, which the authors have tried to present in these pages. We have been particularly concerned to record the features of the landscape which have been the victims of the most recent transitions, but we have also attempted to recapture some of the great events in the history of the city, such as the launching of the *Great Britain* and the construction of Clifton Bridge. We hope, above all, to convey the impression of a living city changing in response to the continuing forces of industrial and social development, and we trust that those who know Bristol will regard it as a fair portrayal.

The book is arranged to deal with various aspects of an interlocking pattern. Beginning with a panoramic view of Bristol at different periods, it goes on to consider the development of the central area, the role of the port and its traffic in the life of Bristol, the various industries which have left their mark on its landscape, and the network of transport systems centred on Bristol. It closes by examining the history of the routes westwards from Bristol to Wales, culminating in the completion of the Severn Bridge.

Bristol in 1717 with Bristol Bridge on the right, St Mary Redcliff church in the left foreground and the cathedral on the extreme left beyond the river

PANORAMA

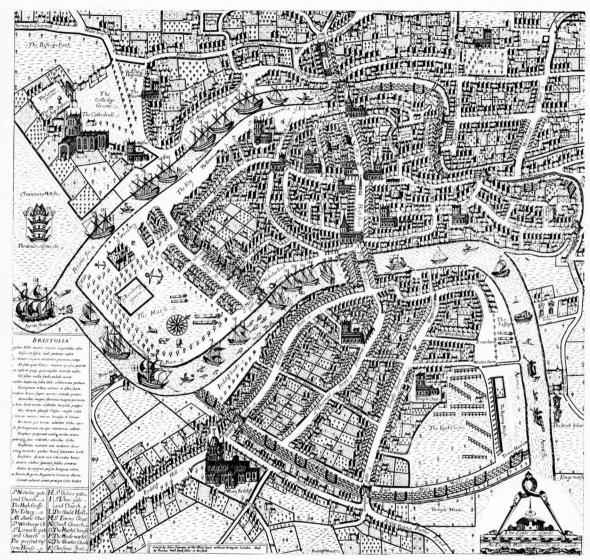

Part of James Millerd's plan of Bristol published in 1673. It illustrates clearly the extent of the harbour and the city of Bristol with Redcliff to the south. The plan also shows the remaining walls of the city and the position of the gates. The site of the castle, destroyed in 1656, had already been developed by the 1670s

Such was the prosperity of Bristol in the Middle Ages that it expanded into the neighbouring marshes, altering the course of the River Frome to provide a greatly improved harbour, and assimilating the adjoining township of Redcliff. From Broad Quay on the Frome, John Cabot set sail in 1497 to inaugurate a new period in the mercantile wealth of the city, based upon trade with the American colonies. In the Civil War of the seventeenth century, Bristol was the greatest prize outside London, and was the subject of fierce competition until the Parliamentary forces gained control. By the eighteenth century, the city had acquired a commanding place in the slave trade across the Atlantic and reached the peak of its ascendancy in the West Country. On the hills to the north of the city, a wealthy and fashionable suburb had sprung up at Clifton and Hotwells, and the industries of Bristol had spread up the valleys of the Frome and Avon, and into the thriving coalfield of Kingswood Forest.

The impact of the Industrial Revolution was not so harsh on Bristol as on some other cities, but it was nonetheless great. The construction of the Floating Harbour made a significant improvement in the port at the beginning of the nineteenth century, and a generation later I. K. Brunel brought the Great Western Railway to Bristol. Many industries took advantage of the excellent transport facilities and the natural resources of the area in order to develop in and around Bristol. The population grew steadily, swelling out into new suburbs on all sides, and absorbing villages which had once been separate. This process continued in the twentieth century, with new industries such as aircraft manufacture and petro-chemicals making their home in the area. Thus, even though Bristol has had periods of comparative stagnation, the dominant trend of its thousand-year history has been one of gradual growth and increasing prosperity.

Coat of arms of the City of Bristol from James Millerd's map

DRAWBRIDGE   PRINCE ST. BRIDGE   BATHURST BASIN   FRY'S FACTORY   WELSH BACK GRANARY   BRISTOL BRIDGE   BEDMINSTER BRIDGE   FINZEL'S SUGAR REFINERY   ST. PHILIPS BRIDGE   PROCTOR'S GLASS CONE

Lavar's view of Bristol, 1887

CHRISTOPHER THOMAS
SOAP WORKS

PHOENIX
GLASSWORKS

ST PHILIPS
STATION

CATTLE
MARKET

TEMPLE MEADS
STATION

Part of a panoramic view of Bristol from the south published by Lavar in 1887 to commemorate Queen Victoria's silver jubilee. Little is known about how this lithograph was prepared but the remarkable accuracy of detail suggests that it could have been based on photographs taken from a balloon

Central Bristol from Perry Road

These two views are sections of a panoramic photograph from the vicinity of Perry Road. The photograph is undated, but was probably taken in the 1920s. Judging from the quality of the light and the comparative freedom from smoke, it was taken on a Sunday afternoon in summer

The section on the left-hand page shows the church towers of Christ Church (City), St Mary-le-Port, and All Saints in the middle distance, with the chimneys of Christopher Thomas' soap factory, the Tramways generating station, Phoenix glass works, and Temple Back generating station, from left to right behind them

The section on the right-hand page shows the tower of St Stephen's church in the left foreground and the spire of St Mary Redcliff in the background. Also, from left to right, note Proctor's glass cone, Welsh Back granary, and Redcliff shot tower

Modern Bristol from the air

Central Bristol showing the Floating Harbour and the arm of the River Frome. Across the foreground is the course of the New Cut, completed as part of William Jessop's improvement works in 1809

The upper sections of the Frome arm of the Floating Harbour were culverted and decked over in the 1890s and 1930s to provide the City Centre of modern Bristol. The statue of Neptune stands at the present head of the Frome (centre foreground). The ancient city wall ran to the left of Baldwin Street (extreme left), and Queen Square (right centre) was developed on the old Town Marsh

THE HEART OF THE CITY

The granary on Welsh Back, completed in 1869 to the designs of Ponton and Gough, is an outstanding example of the unique architectural style which grew up in Bristol in the latter half of the nineteenth century

The original city wall of Bristol enclosed the summit of the sandstone hill upon which the castle and its surrounding buildings had been crowded. The diversion of the Frome in the mid-thirteenth century, from its old confluence with the Avon near Bristol Bridge to its present position, enabled the city to expand southwards beyond Baldwin Street. It also provided a new set of excellent quays on the Frome which became the focal point of commercial activity in the port until the nineteenth century. By this time, the Abbey Church of St Augustine had been absorbed in the city to become the Cathedral Church, and the growth of Clifton had brought a further shift of emphasis towards the western side of the city, although this had been offset to some extent by the development of King Street and Queen Square in the old Town Marsh, and by the intensive industrialisation in Redcliff and St Philip's Marsh. The traditional heart of the city may thus be described as the rectangle within the arms of the Frome and the Avon, bounded by The Grove on the south and the line of Broad Street and High Street on the north.

Broad Quay in the early eighteenth century, by an unknown artist. Note the use of sledges for carrying goods, the hand cranes and the blackamoor (centre foreground)

PERSPECTIVE VIEW OF THE DRAW-BRIDGE, QUAY & CLARE STREE
with the Towers of St. Stephen, Warburgh, All Saints and Christ-Church, Bristol.

St Augustine's Parade and the drawbridge—by this date a swingbridge—in the late 1860s. Irish boats of the Bristol General Steam Navigation Company are moored at Broad Quay

The figurehead of the ss *Demarara* was a distinctive feature of the Quayhead until the 1930s. The ship, one of the largest then built, was wrecked in the Avon in 1851 while being towed to the Clyde to have her engines fitted

The River Frome

(Facing page, above) The quays around the drawbridge formed the heart of Bristol's harbour in the eighteenth century. The prominent tower is of St Stephen's church. (Below) Coastal shipping moored above the drawbridge

Redcliff Back and The Grove

Redcliff was a rival to Bristol until absorbed by it in the thirteenth century. In its splendid parish church of St Mary it has a building worthy of being a cathedral, and easily the most beautiful church in the city. It also has two other ancient and distinguished churches in St Thomas and Temple parishes. Apart from these buildings, however, Redcliff has been a predominantly industrial area, with the manufacture of woollen cloth, glass, pottery, and lead shot, to name only the most famous processes, intimately associated with the district.

The harbour of Redcliff, downstream from Bristol Bridge and under the sandstone cliff which turned the Avon westwards at Redcliff Parade, is now known as Redcliff Back and is cut in half by the twentieth-century Redcliff Bridge. At the end of the cliff, where the Malago Brook once entered the Avon, driving the wheels of Trim Mill as it did so, Bathurst Basin was constructed as part of the Floating Harbour scheme in 1804-9. Opposite Redcliff Back is The Grove, once a set of inlets or 'mud docks' in which ships were berthed to be refitted. The necessary powerful lighting apparatus was provided here, in the eighteenth century, by the 'Great Crane' designed by 'the ingenious Mr Padmore' (see plate p 38). With the increase in the size of ships and the completion of the Floating Harbour, The Grove became an ordinary wharf.

Redcliff Back and The Grove from Benjamin
Donne's map, 1826

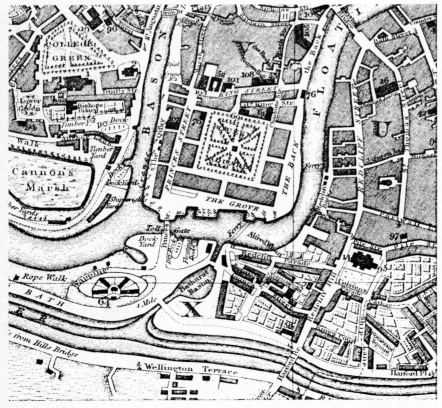

View from Redcliff Parade towards Prince Street Bridge, c 1870. The bridge was then a double-leaf swingbridge. In the left foreground at Lucas Wharf (now Bathurst Wharf) the Guineaman *Look Out* is lying partially dismantled. Opposite, at The Grove is the Nova Scotia barque *Emma Parker* whilst beyond her in the Mud Dock is a Spanish barque from Havana

These two photographs continue the panoramic view from Redcliff Parade begun on the previous page. On the left are the trees of Queen Square and in front the buildings along The Grove. The Sailor's Home is still substantially the same; to the right is the 'Coach and Horses' now part of the 'Hole in the Wall'. The spy hole can be seen at the right of the building. The wooden barque is the West India trader *Maria* probably unloading sugar. Note the hand cranes on the quay

Looking further up the Floating Harbour towards Bristol Bridge. On the left is the roof of the granary recently completed to the designs of Archibald Ponton and William Venn Gough. In the centre distance is the ss *Princess Alexandra* whilst in the foreground at King's Wharf is the Guineaman *Burns* lying outside an unidentified ship. Across the harbour beside the transit shed lies a barque with main top and topgallant masts down. She is possibly the *Orchid* which had recently encountered a hurricane on her voyage from the West Indies

Commercial Architecture

(Above) The round headed arches and subdued polychromy of Bush's warehouse, built as a tea bond in the late 1830s, preceded the exotic style of later dockside architecture in Bristol. (Below) The basement of the General Hospital, designed by William Bruce Gingell, originally provided warehouse accommodation for the Bathurst Basin

Detail of the Welsh Back granary completed in 1869. It is now a jazz club

Warehouse facades on Bathurst Basin. The ogee arches and multi-coloured brickwork were once common in commercial Bristol

PORT AND SHIPS

The steam tug *Bristolian*

Ships and Bristol have always gone together. The early port developed around Bristol Bridge and expanded with the thirteenth-century improvements of the Frome Harbour. The great tidal range of the Avon—it is over forty feet, one of the largest in the world—was initially an advantage to the port, as the ebb and flow of the tide helped ships to make the tortuous ten-mile journey between Bristol and the sea. By the eighteenth century, however, the increasing volume of traffic and the growth in the size of ships had converted this asset into a disadvantage. Shipowners, in particular, objected to the rough treatment received by their vessels in the twice-daily stranding on the mud and rock of the river bed, which could seriously weaken a loaded ship in the days when timber was still the only available constructional material. Attempts had been made to provide enclosed docks at Sea Mills and at the Merchants' Dock in Hotwells, but these had been commercial failures because they were too far from the centre of the city. Many plans for a more radical scheme of port improvement were considered, and since 1800 the port has been twice transformed.

The first occasion was the construction of the Floating Harbour in 1804-9, when the Bristol Dock Company put into effect a scheme prepared by William Jessop, one of the most distinguished civil engineers of the period. Jessop's scheme involved making the course of the River Avon from Rownham Meads to Bristol Bridge, and the River Frome up to the Stone Bridge, into an enclosed freshwater dock, with entrances through Cumberland Basin and Bathurst Basin. The water was kept fresh by supplying it only from the River Frome and from the Avon above Netham weir by way of the Feeder Canal, while the tidal waters of the Avon were diverted into a 'New Cut' between Rownham and Totterdown. The enclosed courses of the old rivers became known as the 'Floating Harbour' because they enabled ships to be kept afloat at all stages of the tide.

Although the enormous engineering tasks necessary to carry through this scheme were completed satisfactorily in five years, the enterprise took longer and cost much more than the Dock Company had envisaged. The result was that the company operated under conditions of acute financial stringency for many years, and that it was obliged to impose high harbour dues in an effort to recover its losses. In addition, it soon became apparent that the growth in the size of ships had not stopped in the eighteenth century, and when the era of large steam ships began in the middle of the nineteenth century the port of Bristol once more became inadequate to deal with the new class of vessel. Thus came the realisation that the future of the port of Bristol depended upon the acquisition of deep-water docks easily accessible from the Severn estuary, which led to the construction of docks at Avonmouth and Portishead, opened in 1877 and 1879 respectively. The result of this further transformation of the port has been to concentrate all large traffic at the mouth of the Avon, keeping the City Docks of the Floating Harbour for a dwindling number

of smaller ships. The trade of the upper part of the Floating Harbour has fallen away so much that a large section of the ancient Frome Harbour has been covered over to make the modern City Centre. The only regular traffic above Prince Street Bridge is now confined to sand and gravel boats. Prince's Wharf, however, is still active in the Baltic timber trade, although it is now anticipated that the whole Floating Harbour will close down within the next ten years. The shift of the port of Bristol to the mouth of the Avon will then be complete, and the city will have to decide what to do with an important industrial monument in the shape of the Floating Harbour.

The Age of Sail

The three-masted barque *Stratford* built at Williamsburg in 1850. She is seen here unloading timber at the Baltic wharf

Wooden three-masted barque *Franziska* under tow in the Avon Gorge near Bridge Valley Road

The *Glaucus*, a steel four-masted barque, at Hotwells

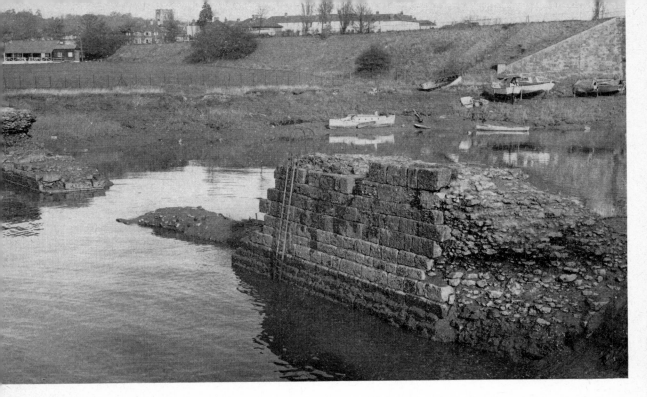

Up the Avon

(Above) Sea Mills dock at the confluence of the River Trym and the Avon. Completed in the early 1700s to the designs of John Padmore, Sea Mills was the third wet dock in Britain. (Below) Pill on the Somerset bank of the Avon was the traditional home of Bristol pilots whose cutters are seen here moored in the creek

(Above) The steam packets *George IV* and *St Patrick* in the Avon above Hotwells, c 1820. (Below) Breaking up a steamship on the banks of the Avon in the 1890s. In the background is the Hotwells terminus of the Bristol Port Railway and Pier Company

Cumberland Basin

(Above) Cumberland Basin from Rownham Hill, in the 1880s. Ships are entering through the new lock completed in 1873. On the right is the Brunel lock and the blocked up remains of Jessop's north entrance lock. (Below) Water-colour of the Overfall dam showing water from the Floating Harbour flowing into the New Cut, by T. W. Rowbotham, 1827. The Underfall now occupies this site

Cumberland Basin and entrance locks to the City Docks, 1966. In the left foreground is the Underfall Yard; to the right Merchants' Dock is being filled. The sections of the new fly-over are named after great engineers associated with Bristol, such as McAdam, Brunel, and Davy, while the swinging central section (closed in this picture) is named Plimsoll Bridge after Samuel Plimsoll who was born in Bristol in 1824

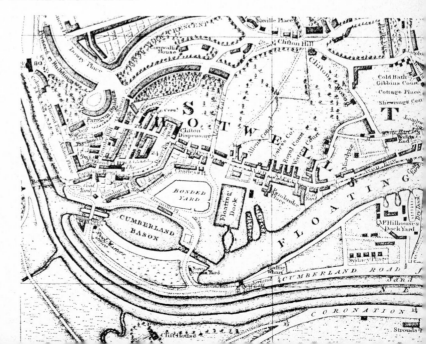

The Cumberland Basin area as it appeared on Donne's map of 1826

Brunel and Bristol Docks

(Above) I. K. Brunel's entrance lock to Cumberland Basin, completed in 1848. The single-leaf iron caisson gate fitted into the curved masonry recess when open. The lock is now blocked by a concrete wall with sluice gates. (Below) The wrought-iron girder swingbridge designed by Brunel to span his new entrance lock. This was the first use of tubular girders by Brunel

(Above) As one of his contributions to solving the problem of silting in the harbour, Brunel designed a type of drag-boat which scraped mud from the sides of locks and basins so that it could be removed by conventional dredging. One such boat was the *BD6*, built in 1843 and in regular service until 1961. The boom on the right is the head of the spade or scraper. (Below) Brunel's first ship was the wooden paddle steamer *Great Western* launched from Patterson's yard, Bristol in 1837. She was the first steam vessel built specifically for the North Atlantic service

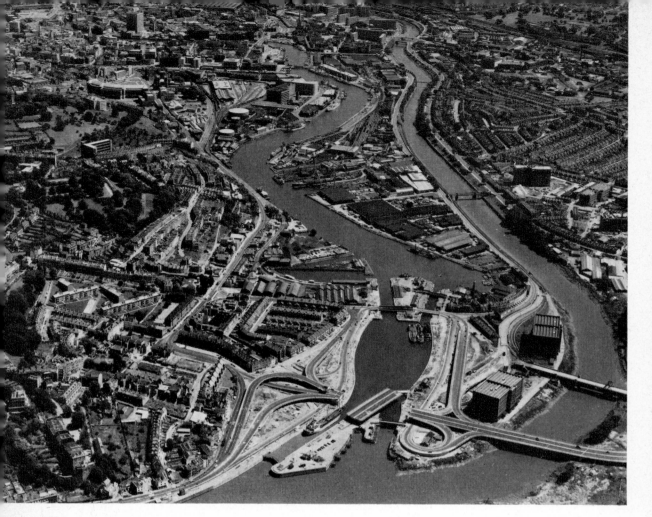

The Floating Harbour

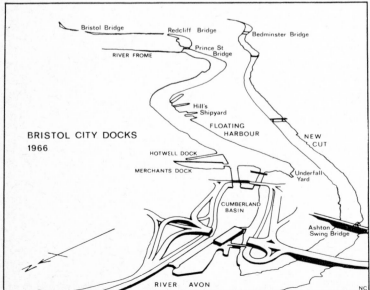

BRISTOL CITY DOCKS
1966

Bristol Bridge

Redcliff Bridge

Bedminster Bridge

Prince St Bridge

RIVER FROME

Hill's Shipyard

FLOATING HARBOUR

NEW CUT

HOTWELL DOCK

MERCHANTS DOCK

Underfall Yard

CUMBERLAND BASIN

Ashton Swing Bridge

RIVER AVON

NC

City Docks and the New Cut, 1966

(Above) Limekiln dock in 1826 with Brandon Hill in the background, by T. W. Rowbotham. (Below) Filling Limekiln dock in the early 1900s prior to the construction of the railway to the new goods depot at Canon's Marsh

THE Great Crane at the Gibb of Bristol ERECTED By Mr John Cadmore In the year 17[...]

The 'Great Crane of Bristol' erected in 1735 at the Gibb near the end of Prince Street. Designed by John Padmore it was probably powered by large treadmills

STEAM "FAIRBAIRN" CRANE.

FIG. 149.
(Engraved from a Photograph of a 35-Ton Crane erected at the Bristol Docks.)

THIS type of Crane was originally introduced by the late Sir William Fairbairn (hence its title), and is considered the best form of Crane for dealing with heavy and bulky packages in and out of high-sided vessels of large beam and tonnage, giving, as it does, the greatest possible amount of clearance under the jib sheave.

The Crane illustrated, had a radius of 35 feet from the centre to the plumb of the chain, and a height of 49 feet from ground line to the centre of the jib head sheave, and was constructed for lifting loads up to 35 tons.

London Office.—CORNES, CALVERT & Co., 30, Walbrook, E.C.

Heavy-lift crane installed on Wapping wharf by Messrs Stothert & Pitt in the 1870s. This 35-ton steam crane is still in occasional use

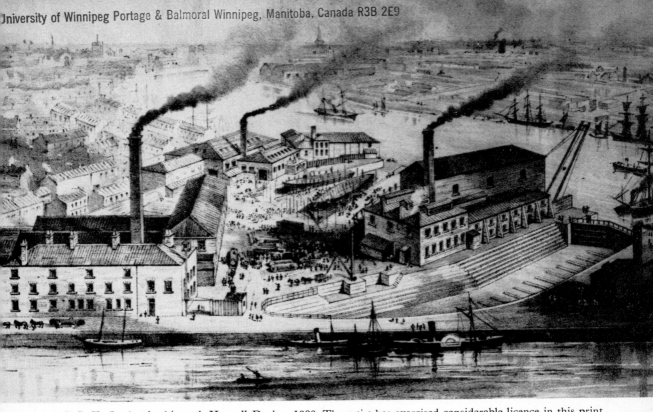

(Above) G. K. Stothert's shipyard, Hotwell Dock, c 1900. The artist has exercised considerable licence in this print, particularly in representing a river in the foreground, where there should be a road. (Below) The launch of the sand boat *Norleader* on 24 February 1967 from the Albion shipyard of Charles Hill & Sons. This was one of the last ships to be built in Bristol

Trows and Tugs

(Above) The hull of the trow *Safety*, built at Stourport in 1838, lies derelict on the bank of the New Cut. In the background is Ashton Swing Bridge. (Below) Model of the Severn trow *Alma* built at Gloucester in 1854, showing the fore-and-aft rig typical in the nineteenth century

(Above) Brown's steam tug *Medway* built in the 1890s leaves Avonmouth on 14 September 1965 on her last voyage, to the breakers at Newport. (Below) King's tugs *Merrimac* and *Bristolian*, the last of the old generation of steam tugs, bring a ship into Avonmouth

LAUNCH OF THE
Great Britain
GRAND STAND.
THE
BEST SIGHT

For Viewing the above, will be from the

BALLAST-WHARF, HOTWELL-ROAD,
Immediately Opposite the Head of the Ship,
WHERE THE BEST ACCOMMODATION MAY BE HAD.

For Tickets of Admission apply to Mr. SLOCOMBE, Builder, at the Wharf, or at his Yard, Cave-Street, Portland-Square.

SOMERTON, PRINTER, BRISTOL MERCURY-OFFICE

'Great Britain'

Brunel's second ship, *Great Britain*, was the first large vessel to be built of iron and the first to be screw propelled. She was built in a specially constructed dry dock—which still exists—and was floated into the harbour after the 'launch' by HRH Prince Albert on 19 July 1843

This view by Fox-Talbot, one of the pioneers of modern photography, was taken in 1844 when *Great Britain* was lying at Hotwells prior to leaving Bristol for the first and last time

Today *Great Britain* lies in Sparrow Cove near Port Stanley in the Falkland Islands although efforts are being made to preserve her and to bring her back to Bristol

Docks at Avonmouth

(Above) Construction of the Royal Edward Dock, Avonmouth, in the early 1900s. (Below) The royal yacht *Victoria & Albert* leaves Avonmouth after the opening of the Royal Edward Dock in 1908

Modern Avonmouth. A view over the Eastern Arm of the Royal Edward Dock in November 1968. General cargo ships, with the Port of Bristol's No 5 Granary (30,000 tons capacity, opened in 1966) in the background

INDUSTRY

TOWERS OF REDCLIFF. The shot tower, in the foreground, has been recently demolished, but the graceful edifice of St Mary Redcliff may also be regarded as an industrial monument as it was built largely from the profits of the woollen cloth industry

The industries of Bristol have always been varied, and they have constantly changed to adapt to new phases in the life of the city. In the Middle Ages, the woollen cloth industry was important, providing employment for some of the largest craft guilds in Bristol. Other crafts, such as cooperage and rope-making, were associated with the port and the needs of its ships or with the commodities brought into the city through its foreign trade. Soap-making was another early industry, and one of the first to take advantage of the coal from Kingswood Forest.

It was in Kingswood, to the east of the city, that the seams of the Bristol Coalfield were most accessible. In time, however, it was discovered that the coal measures stretched right under the city and on both sides of the Avon into Gloucestershire and Somerset. At the height of its activity, in the late nineteenth century, coal was being mined intensively throughout this region, although the coal mining industry has now dwindled to a handful of pits around Radstock. Local coal was the essential fuel for a range of industrial processes in and around Bristol, such as lead-smelting, brass-working, glass-making and the manufacture of pottery. Plantation crops became the basis of important Bristol industries with the development of transatlantic trade in the eighteenth century. Particularly significant in this respect were the sugar, tobacco, and cocoa industries, with cotton being a late starter in the middle of the nineteenth century.

The tendency of industries to grow into ever larger enterprises in the twentieth century has resulted in the extinction of some famous Bristol industries such as glass and sugar. Others, however, like tobacco, have grown and retained their roots in the city, and these have been joined by important new industries in engineering, chemicals, and paper processing. Diversity remains the predominant characteristic of the pattern of Bristol industry, even though the main location of manufacturing enterprises has shifted from the traditional centres in Redcliff, St Philip's Marsh, and the Crews Hole valley, towards Severnside, the aircraft engineering complex at Filton, and the new trading estates in the suburbs. Despite the many changes in its industrial history, therefore, Bristol has always been an important centre of manufacturing industry.

Ashton mill, Chapel Allerton. Restored in 1958 by Mr C. C. Clarke, the mill is now maintained by Bristol City Museum

Coal

(Above) Middle Pit, Radstock, was abandoned in 1930, but the chimney and some of the buildings survive. It was one of the many collieries which once flourished in the Somerset Coalfield, of which only two are still operating. (Below) The old steam winding engine at Kilmersdon colliery, built by William Evans of Paulton Foundry in 1875. It was scrapped in 1966

Iron

(Above) The Bathurst Basin ironworks in the early nineteenth century with Guinea Street on the left. The site is now occupied by the General Hospital. (Below) Cast-iron buildings, mainly for export, were made in large numbers at the ironworks of Samuel Hemming, Clift House, Bristol. This view (1854) shows a prefabricated church assembled prior to export

Lead

(Above) St Cuthbert's lead works, Priddy, was the last to smelt lead on Mendip. This photograph probably dates from soon after the closure of the works in 1908. The chimneys have now disappeared and the other buildings have been reduced to rubble. (Below) Condensing flues at Charterhouse-on-Mendip lead works in 1966

Redcliff Hill shot tower, Bristol. This first shot tower in the world was built in the late 1780s and demolished in autumn 1968

Engraved lead plate beside the main entrance of the shot tower

Brass

This building is the most substantial relic of the large brass works established at Warmley in the mid-eighteenth century by William Champion, a Bristol Quaker and prominent industrialist of the period. The blocks of black copper slag incorporated in the building were a by-product of the industry and can be found in abundance in those parts of the Bristol region where the brass industry flourished

Remnants of the brass industry also survive at Keynsham, Saltford, and Kelston. This is one of the two annealing ovens at Kelston Mills

Glass

(Above) The Cathay Chemical Works of H. & T. Proctor in the 1850s. The cone in the centre was built in the late eighteenth century for glassmaking. (Below) The base of the cone still stands, the only survivor of many in Bristol, and may be preserved

Soap

The soap factory of Christopher Thomas & Bros was built in the early 1880s. The architecture was inspired by that of Florence, although the ornate chimney has now disappeared and the corner turrets of the main building have been truncated. The building is in Broad Plain. It stopped producing soap in the 1950s

Pottery

Good quality pottery has been produced in the Bristol region since the Brislington Pottery first made 'Bristol delft' in 1652, but the one remaining firm in the business, Pountneys Bristol Pottery, has announced plans to leave the city in the near future. This view shows the present factory at Fishponds

Sugar

Conrad Finzel's sugar refinery on the Counterslip, Bristol, was one of the largest in the country at the peak of its prosperity in the 1860s. The site is now occupied by George's brewery

Wool

Of all the many remains of the once-great woollen cloth industry in the Bristol region, those of the Dunkirk Mill at Freshford are amongst the most complete. The shell of the derelict building still looks like it does on this copper token issued in 1795

Cotton

The Great Western cotton factory beside the Feeder Canal in Barton Hill employed over 1,000 people when it was opened in 1837. This view shows the five-storey spinning block with the weaving sheds alongside. Later used for artificial fibre manufacture and then as a warehouse, the main building was demolished early in 1968

Chocolate

The chocolate factory of J. S. Fry & Sons in Pithay about 1924, shortly before the firm moved out of central Bristol to Somerdale. The whole of this site has now been redeveloped, leaving no trace of its intensive industrial occupation of fifty years ago. The road junction in the foreground is that between Wine Street and Union Street

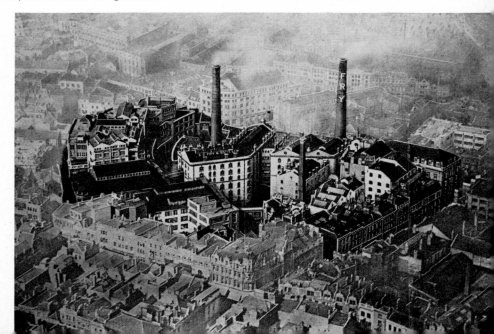

Chemicals

The valley of the Avon at Crews Hole attracted many noxious industrial processes in the eighteenth and nineteenth centuries, but has since been largely abandoned. There was an important alkali factory at Netham (foreground), and there is still a tar distillery higher up the valley. An early tar distilling plant was responsible for the flue up the side of Troopers Hill to the chimney which still stands gauntly on the summit

Many lesser chemical processes have flourished at various times in the Bristol region. Albert Mill at Keynsham, for example, manufactured dyes from logwood until quite recently

Paper and Board

The packaging and printing business of E. S. & A. Robinson began in a shop in Baldwin Street in 1844. In 1846 the business moved to its present site in the angle of Redcliff Street and Victoria Street. The building in this photograph was the administrative block which was destroyed by fire and rebuilt in 1903. It was severely damaged by bombing in 1941 and was demolished in 1961 to make way for the new fifteen-storey office block. The frieze round the middle of the tower represents the various stages of paper-making and has been preserved

A detail from the frieze. The stonework has been dismantled and awaits re-erection

St Anne's Board Mill has expanded vigorously in recent years on this site where the Avon emerges from the Crews Hole valley. It has engulfed the old Brislington Pottery, which in turn stood upon the site of the medieval chapel of St Anne. The largest of the three chimneys is 300 ft high and was built in 1961

Tobacco

Snuffy Jack's Mill in Stapleton Glen around 1926. Many Bristol watermills were converted to snuff-grinding at the end of the eighteenth century, when snuff was in fashion. Part of the building has been preserved in Snuff Mills Park, with a waterwheel *in situ*

Tobacco shop in Mary-le-Port Street, probably in the 1890s, as this timber-framed building was demolished in 1904. Note the familiar trade names

(Above) Three large tobacco bonds are a prominent feature of the Ashton Gate area of Bristol. This view shows 'A' warehouse, an iron-frame structure completed in 1905. 'B' warehouse of 1908 was the first large concrete-frame building in Britain to be built on the Coignet principle. (Below) Further concrete tobacco bonds dating from the 1920s tower over Canon's Marsh

Gas

Canon's Marsh gas works, now semi-derelict. The office building on the left dates from the 1820s

Water

Chelvey pumping station opened by Bristol Waterworks in 1923. The building still houses a triple-expansion vertical steam engine made by the Lilleshall Company

Electricity

The Central Electric Lighting Station was Bristol's first power station, completed in 1893. In the background is the tramway company generating station beside St Philips bridge, opened in 1904

Modern Industry

This 260 ft high building in the commercial centre of Bristol is the headquarters of the Dickinson Robinson stationery and packaging group. It was designed by the group's own architects, and when it was completed in 1963 it was one of the first fully air-conditioned office buildings in Britain

Although the Redcliff shot tower had to be demolished in the interests of road improvement, there has been no change in the essentially simple process of manufacturing lead shot by allowing molten lead to fall from a height. For all its modernity, therefore, the new shot tower in Cheese Lane operates on the same principle. Built in 1968 for Sheldon Bush & Patent Shot Co by E. N. Underwood & Partners, the new tower is 141 ft high

TRANSPORT

A train from Avonmouth to Hotwells on the line of the Bristol Port Railway & Pier Company. The extension to Hotwells was closed in 1922 and much of the alignment disappeared when the Portway was built

Bristol enjoys an unparalleled position as the hub of the transport system of the South West. The old Great West Road led out of London, over the Marlborough Downs, and down through Bath to Bristol, where it linked with roads from Gloucester, Bridgwater, and the Old Ferry at Aust, from which it was possible to make a crossing to Wales. The intersection of the projected motorways M4 and M5 at Almondsbury, just to the north of Bristol, epitomises the continuing importance of the city in the national network of modern roads.

With the coming of the railways, there was the same conjunction of routes at Bristol. Brunel's Great Western Railway came sweeping down with its seven-foot gauge, through the Box Tunnel from Paddington, and then along the Avon valley from Bath to Bristol. In a field in Temple parish, Brunel built the splendid terminus to his railway which still stands as Old Temple Meads, with its functional wooden-arched train shed and ornate offices on Temple Gate, the oldest surviving complete railway terminus in the world. The Bristol & Exeter Railway carried on the rail route to the West, while the Midland Railway brought the link with the North, and the opening of the Severn Tunnel in 1886 completed the main railway pattern of the Bristol region.

Bristol had less need of canals than most British cities, particularly after the Avon had been made navigable for barges as far as Bath in 1727. The city did have an interest, however, in the extension of the waterway eastwards to the Thames by way of the Kennet & Avon Canal, completed by the distinguished engineer and architect John Rennie in 1810. Although several other canal schemes were discussed for the region, the only one to be completed was the Somersetshire Coal Canal, linking the coal mines of North Somerset with the Kennet & Avon Canal at the Dundas Aqueduct.

Seal of the Great Western Railway Company

Roads

The Bristol Turnpike Trust became the largest turnpike authority in the country during the 1820s, when J. L. McAdam was the Surveyor of Bristol Roads. It had some 180 miles of road in its care, and many road-side relics survive from this period of road development. This cast-iron signpost, at the junction of the Bath and Wells roads at Totterdown, is a conspicuous example

Some roads still possess almost complete sets of milestones from the days of the Turnpike Trust. This specimen on the Bridgwater road is an iron casting of a type widely used in the region

(Above) Tollhouse at Prince Street Bridge undermined by shipping. From a pencil sketch by T. W. Rowbotham, 1828. (Below) Ashton Gate tollhouse is the finest building of its kind in Bristol

Railways

The down Bristol Pullman emerging from the west portal of Box Tunnel

The eastern approach of the Great Western Railway into Bath through Sydney Gardens. This lithograph by J. C. Bourne shows the final stages of construction in 1840

Temple Meads in the early 1960s showing the original GWR terminus of 1840 fronting on to Temple Gate and the present main-line station on the curve to the right. The line of the Bristol Harbour Railway, opened in 1872, is to the left of the station, and beyond it the covered goods depot

(Above) The Great Western terminated in a magnificent timber-roofed train shed at Temple Meads, Bristol. Although now used as a car park the building is still substantially as Bourne depicted it in this illustration of the 1840s. (Below) The neo-Tudor facade of Brunel's original terminus building has been little altered. It is now threatened with demolition for road widening

(Above) Temple Meads in the 1860s. Brunel's train shed of the Great Western terminus provides a sharp contrast with the crude wooden buildings on the left used by the Bristol & Exeter Railway. The B & ER offices are in the distance. (Below) Passengers transferring from the Great Western Railway to the steamship *Great Western* were provided for by the Royal Western Hotel, designed by R. S. Pope. The building, now 'Brunel House', still stands behind the Council House

Steam engine installed in 1872 to operate the bascule bridge carrying the Bristol Harbour Railway over the entrance to Bathurst Basin

Bathurst Basin bascule bridge in 1964 shortly before demolition

A broad gauge carriage body formed the first Wesleyan mission room in Portbury

IN 1892, ISAMBARD KINGDOM BRUNEL'S BROAD-GAUGE RAILWAY SYSTEM, (G.W.R.) WAS REPLACED BY THE STANDARD GAUGE OF 4'8½".

- THIS BROAD-GAUGE RAILWAY CARRIAGE WAS USED FOR SEVERAL YEARS AS THE 'PORTBURY WESLEYAN MISSION ROOM' AT THE SITE OF THE PRESENT WATER WORKS, BY THE RAILWAY STATION. IT WAS TOWED TO ITS PRESENT SITUATION BY Mr E.H.SHOPLAND, & HIS GOOD HORSE "SMART," ON THE ERECTION OF THE PRESENT CHURCH IN 1899.

The Avon & Gloucestershire Railway

The north entrance to Willsbridge tunnel on the Avon & Gloucestershire Railway, c 1900. Opened in 1832, the A & GR carried coal from pits in the Mangotsfield area to the River Avon. The north section was closed in the 1860s but that south of California pit survived until 1904

Londonderry wharf on the Avon was one of the two southern termini of the A & GR. The bridge on the left crosses the mouth of the Siston Brook. The building was a weighhouse

Alignment of the A & GR crossing Siston Common

Stone sleeper block *in situ* on Oldland Common

Waterways

(Above) Totterdown lock gave direct access to the Feeder Canal and to the head of the Floating Harbour at the point where the tidal water of the Avon had been diverted into the New Cut. This sketch by H. O'Neill shows the lock in 1821. (Below) The Avon Navigation was opened in 1727 and gave sizeable barges access to Bath. This is Hanham lock in the 1890s

Dundas aqueduct, designed by John Rennie, carried the Kennet & Avon Canal over the River Avon near Claverton. The junction with the Somersetshire Coal Canal is in the foreground

Three miles upstream from the Dundas aqueduct, the Kennet & Avon Canal recrosses the River Avon over the Avoncliff aqueduct. This is not so finely finished as its companion structure, and it has been dry for several years owing to defects in the canal banks

Winsley incline connected stone quarries with the Kennet & Avon Canal. The stone sleeper blocks have recently been covered with tarmacadam

The Somersetshire Coal Canal ran for ten miles up the Midford and Dunkerton valleys to reach the coal mines around Camerton. The canal was at two levels, connected by a remarkable flight of twenty-two locks near Combe Hay. This milepost is one of several along the canal

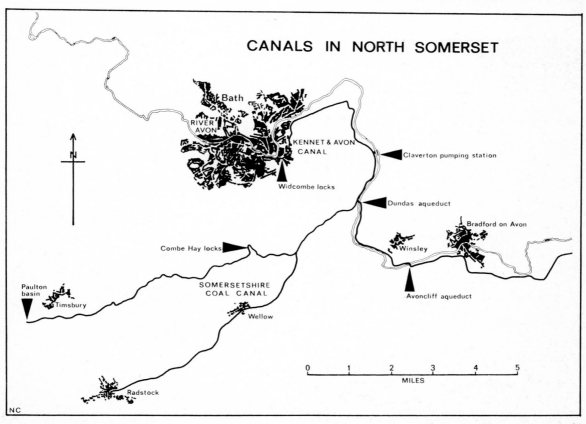

CANALS IN NORTH SOMERSET

Bath

RIVER AVON

KENNET & AVON CANAL

Claverton pumping station

Widcombe locks

Dundas aqueduct

Bradford on Avon

Combe Hay locks

Winsley

Avoncliff aqueduct

Paulton basin

Timsbury

SOMERSETSHIRE COAL CANAL

Wellow

Radstock

NC

0   1   2   3   4   5
MILES

Bristol Trams

(Above) The Tramway Centre in the late 1930s, the hub of Bristol's tramway network. Only open-top trams ran on the system right down to its closure in 1940. (Below) A signal box with semaphore arms controlled trams negotiating the junction of Colston Street and Perry Road

(Above) The tram terminus at Hotwells. Passengers for Clifton continued via the funicular Clifton Rocks Railway until its closure in 1934. (Below) A line-up of new buses built at the Brislington works of the Bristol Tramway & Carriage Company. Note the track and wires for the trams

Made in Bristol

(Above) Locomotive building was an important industry in Bristol until the 1950s. This 2–4–0 wood-burner was built in 1873 by Fox-Walker for the Cordoba & Tucuman Railway in Argentina. (Below) Regular production of 'Bristol' passenger chassis was started in 1913, initially for the Bristol Tramway & Carriage Company's own fleet. Today, as Bristol Commercial Vehicles Ltd, the firm is one of the country's largest bus chassis builders. Here a 2-ton single-decker has a clinometer test at the Brislington works, about 1925

(Above) Sir George White, Chairman of the Bristol Tramways Company, founded the British & Colonial Aeroplane Company (soon to become the Bristol Aeroplane Company) at the Filton terminus of the Bristol trams in 1910. In the same year, the company produced its first successful aeroplane, the *Boxkite*. Here a *Boxkite* is being demonstrated in Denmark. (Below) *Concorde* 002, the second prototype of the Anglo/French supersonic airliner leaves the main aircraft assembly hall at Filton for the first time on 12 September 1968

Day Return to Portishead

(Above) Portishead was a rather isolated village until the construction of the branch line by the Bristol & Portishead Pier & Railway Co, opened in 1867. Portishead Dock followed in 1879, and the village has grown in importance as a dormitory and resort for Bristol. The picture shows the branch line under construction. (Below) Broad gauge Bristol & Exeter Railway 4–4–0 saddle tank locomotive and train at Portishead station, about 1870

(Above) Portishead High Street in the 1890s, with small boys dressed for a decorous day by the seaside. (Below) A returning excursion stops at Clifton Bridge station, some time in the 1890s. Note that the transition to standard gauge track has been completed

CROSSING THE AVON

I. K. Brunel's proposed design for Clifton Suspension Bridge as finally accepted by the Trustees was wholeheartedly Egyptian in style. The towers surmounted by sphinxes, were to be clad in cast-iron bas reliefs illustrating the construction of the bridge. Massive sarcophagi formed a visual termination for the suspension chains

There are now many bridges—road, rail and foot—across the Avon, so that it requires an effort of the imagination to understand the significance of Bristol Bridge at a time when this was the only crossing point between Keynsham and the Severn estuary. Such it was, however, until comparatively recent times, and thus it remains the doyen of Bristol bridges. It is not known when the first bridge was built at this point, but there has certainly been a stone bridge here since the middle of the thirteenth century, when it was constructed as part of the harbour improvement works at that time. The masonry of the present bridge was built in 1768, although it has been subsequently widened and modified.

The excavation of the New Cut in 1804-9 made necessary the construction of two new bridges to carry the Bath and Bridgwater roads out of the city to the south. These were built in cast-iron by the Coalbrookdale Company, but both had to be re-built later in the century. Hill's Bridge, on the Bath Road, was swept away when a barge collided with it in 1855, and Harford's Bridge, at Bedminster, was replaced in 1884. The vast increase of road traffic in the twentieth century has led to the duplication of both bridges to carry dual carriageways.

The age of the railways produced several more bridges across the Avon and the New Cut, including the remarkable double-purpose structure, the Ashton Swing Bridge, with a railway track on the lower and a road on the upper of its two decks. Opened in 1906, this was designed as a swing bridge in order to allow vessels to sail up the New Cut, but the disappearance of this traffic caused the bridge to be fixed. The road deck has been made redundant by the new road scheme at the Cumberland Basin, and has been removed. This new scheme, the Cumberland Basin Swing Bridge, with its complex pattern of fly-overs, is designed to maintain the flow of traffic across the entrances to the Cumberland Basin even when one or other of the swing bridges is open to admit a vessel. It was completed in 1965.

Some attractive foot bridges have been built over the New Cut, and there are now so many bridges of one sort or another that the ferries which once did a thriving trade across the Avon and the New Cut have mostly disappeared, although the road approach to Rownham Ferry is still visible at low tide and traces of other ferries remain. The only ferries which still ply an active trade are those below the Gorge such as Lamplighters Ferry at Pill.

(Above) The medieval Bristol Bridge with its houses and chapel survived until the 1760s. The narrow arches restricted the flow of the river creating a weir effect. (Below) The new bridge completed in 1768/9 was designed by James Bridges. It was widened in 1873

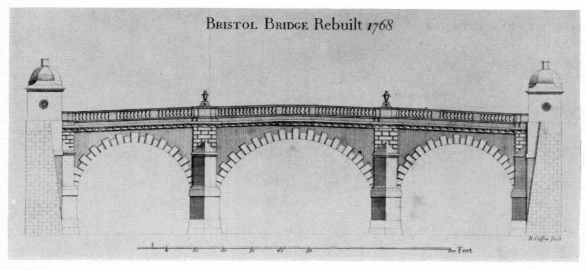

BRISTOL BRIDGE Rebuilt 1768

Bristol Bridge seen from Welsh Back in the 1920s. The chimneys (top left) are those of Fry's factory in Pithay

Bedminster Bridge, supplied in 1806 by the Coalbrookdale Company of Shropshire. There was a similar bridge on the Bath road at Temple Meads. This sketch was made in 1821 by H. O'Neill

Clifton Bridge

(Above) One of the earliest schemes for a bridge across the Avon Gorge was proposed by William Bridges in 1793. Besides the great arch, 220 ft high and 180 ft wide, provision was made for factories, granaries, a corn exchange, and even a library and museum. (Below) Thomas Telford, one of the judges for the 1829 competition, submitted this design for a suspension bridge in the gothic style with towers rising from the bottom of the gorge

The abandoned abutment and tower at Leigh Woods is on the right, before work on the bridge recommenced. The tower in the centre is that of the camera obscura on Clifton Down, which had been a windmill used for snuff-grinding before a fire had destroyed the machinery in 1777. The curious building in the foreground is the water pumping station built at Black Rock by the Society of Merchant Venturers in 1845

A Bristol wine merchant called William Vick bequeathed £1,000 to the Society of Merchant Venturers in 1753, with instructions that it should be allowed to accumulate until it reached the sum of £10,000, which he judged would be adequate to construct a road bridge over the Avon Gorge at Clifton. A committee was set up in 1829 to decide on a design for such a bridge, as a result of which a competition was held with Thomas Telford acting as the adjudicator. The designs which were submitted included some very bizarre ideas and also some which incorporated the most progressive civil engineering conceptions. After much indecision on the part of the committee, the competition was eventually won by the young I. K. Brunel, who was living in Clifton at the time. Work began in 1831 but proceeded very slowly until all the capital was exhausted in the mid-1840s with only the abutments and towers completed. The project remained in this condition until after Brunel's death in 1859, when some of his fellow engineers resolved to finish the bridge as a memorial to the great man. A new company was formed, and the work was at length completed in December 1864, endowing Bristol with one of its best known and most graceful landmarks. The bridge is essentially as Brunel designed it, although some modifications were made after his death such as the decision to use three suspension chains instead of two on each side. It is 702 ft 3 in long between the centres of the two towers, and the roadway is at a height of 245 ft above high water in the Avon. The platform is 31 ft wide (20 ft between the chains), and the towers are 86 ft high to the top of the caps.

(Above) This view from above Rownham Ferry (centre) shows both towers as they stood, almost complete, from being abandoned in the 1840s until work recommenced in 1861. The following pictures show stages in the completion of the bridge. (Below) Work resumed. Scaffolding in position around the towers, and a gangway completed between them. The promontory and many of the buildings of Hotwells Baths were removed in order to improve access to the City Docks a few years later

(Above) The chains are complete, the scaffolding has been removed, and the bridge platform is in an advanced stage of construction. (Below) The finished work, as seen from Clifton Down. The cap to the Clifton tower bears an inscription commemorating I. K. Brunel, who did not live to see the completion of his plans.

Ferries and Bridges

(Above) In its original position Rownham ferry crossed the Avon below the Cumberland Basin entrance locks. This view dating from the 1860s clearly shows the caisson gate of Brunel's 1848 entrance lock. (Below) When the new entrance lock was opened in 1873 Rownham ferry was moved upstream to a point above Brunel's lock. The ferry boat crossed on a cable when the tide was high

At low tide, however, a bridge of boats carried the footpath across the river. These stretches of roadway are still visible, although the ferry closed in 1933. The building in the background is the dockmaster's house

(Above) Ashton Swing Bridge was opened in 1906 with a road on the top deck and a railway below. Originally a signal cabin stood above the road but this and the top deck have now been removed. (Below) Gasworks ferry when the Floating Harbour was frozen

Bristol's mini-suspension bridge, completed in 1935, carries pedestrians across the New Cut near the site of Wapping Gaol

THE ROAD TO WALES

The Severn Bridge viewed from between the two carriageways shortly before the opening ceremony

The wide funnel of the Severn estuary has always been the gateway to the port of Bristol, and the trade of Severnside was for long of vital importance to the mercantile prosperity of the city. While providing a maritime highway, however, the Severn was for many centuries a formidable barrier to the easy movement of travellers between England and South Wales. The width of the estuary, with its great tidal range, shifting sandbanks, and treacherous currents, long made it impossible to bridge and difficult to cross. Nevertheless, crossings had to be made, and so routes had to be found. The 'Old Passage' at Aust, between the cliffs at that point and the Beachley peninsula at the mouth of the Wye, was almost certainly used from Roman times as the most convenient crossing place south of the point where Gloucester now stands. Even here, at one of its narrowest points, the estuary is a mile wide.

The nineteenth century replacement, 'New Passage', was twice as wide. This stretched from a point near Severn Beach to Blackrock at Sudbrook on the opposite shore. It was designed to provide a terminus for a railway which ran out into the estuary on a pier. After a brief period of prosperity, this was made redundant by the Severn Tunnel. The construction of this four-mile-long tunnel was a protracted operation, becoming an epic of civil engineering because of the many difficulties encountered, amongst which the bursting in of the 'Great Spring'—virtually an underground river—was the most severe, only overcome by the installation of batteries of powerful Cornish pumping engines at Severn Beach and Sudbrook. It was completed in 1886, and thereafter it has taken the main rail routes from London and Bristol to South Wales. Another rail crossing of the Severn had meanwhile been made at Sharpness in 1879, by a bridge consisting of twenty-two wrought-iron bowstring girders which was demolished in 1967.

The growth of road traffic in the twentieth century encouraged the search for means of shortening the road route from Bristol to South Wales. A car ferry was opened on the course of the 'Old Passage' and remained in operation until 1966, when the new Severn Bridge came into operation. This beautiful bridge is the culmination of many years of designing and construction. The slim towers are 400 ft high and 3,240 ft apart. The aerodynamically designed platform carries the dual carriageways of the M4, thus providing a vital link in the national motorway network and carrying the modern road to Wales. The bridge was opened by HM Queen Elizabeth II on 8 September 1966, and will stand for long as the symbol of the new Severnside, in the life and industry of which Bristol will continue to have, as it has had in the past, a leading role to perform.

One of the last of the Severn ferries: *Severn King* at Aust landing stage in 1966

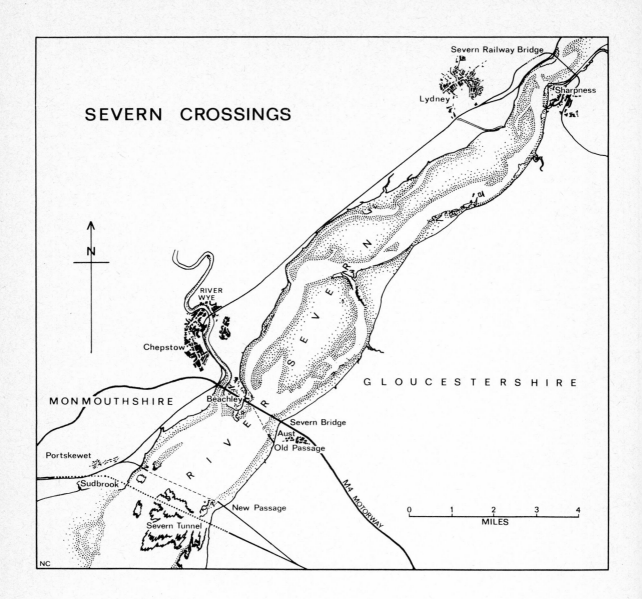

SEVERN CROSSINGS

Severn Railway Bridge

Lydney

Sharpness

N

RIVER WYE

Chepstow

GLOUCESTERSHIRE

MONMOUTHSHIRE

Beachley

Severn Bridge

Aust

Old Passage

Portskewet

Sudbrook

New Passage

M4 MOTORWAY

Severn Tunnel

RIVER SEVERN

0   1   2   3   4
MILES

NC

(Above) The pier at New Passage on the opening day of the Bristol & South Wales Union Railway, 8 September 1863. (Below) New Passage Hotel in 1966. The stump of the pier still remains adjacent to the hotel

Severn tunnel engine house over the 29 ft diameter shaft at Sudbrook

The beams of the six Cornish engines installed at Sudbrook in 1886

(Above) Dismantling of the Severn Bridge at Sharpness, September 1967. (Below) Old Passage ferry. Cars wait at Beachley under the shadow of the suspension bridge, August 1966

A vital link in the new motorway network, the Almondsbury intersection begins to take shape. A short stretch of the M5 brings in traffic from Bristol to the right, but work has not yet started on the link with Birmingham to the left. The M4 comes from Tormarton, ten miles on the way to London, and continues over the Severn Bridge to Newport

The Severn Bridge, linking Bristol with South Wales more effectively than they have ever been linked before, is a hopeful symbol for the future development and prosperity of both sides of the Severn estuary

BIBLIOGRAPHICAL NOTE

This book may be read as a complementary volume to another work by the same authors:

Buchanan, R. A. and Cossons, Neil : *Industrial Archaeology of the Bristol Region.* Newton Abbot, 1969

The industrial archaeology book is able to explore in depth themes which can only be touched briefly in the present work : there are chapters on the port, the leading industries of the region, the transport systems, and the public services, dealing with each of these subjects from the point of view of its industrial history and physical remains. The book is well illustrated with a completely different selection of photographs from those used in this collection. There are also appendixes covering such subjects as the railway chronology of the region, and a comprehensive list of industrial archaeological sites in and around Bristol.

For a brief guide to industrial archaeological sites in the region, a convenient summary will be found in:

Cossons, Neil.   *Industrial Monuments in the Mendip, South Cotswold and Bristol Region*
Bristol Archaeological Research Group, Field Guide No 4, 1967

On a similar scale, there is a useful introduction to the subject in:

Buchanan, R. A.   *The Industrial Archaeology of Bristol*
Bristol Branch of the Historical Association, pamphlet No 18, 1967

This is one of a series containing several pamphlets relevant to the industrial history of Bristol, including:

Sherborne, J. W.   *The Port of Bristol in the Middle Ages.* 1965
Minchinton, Walter.   *The Port of Bristol in the Eighteenth Century.* 1962
Farr, Grahame.   *The Steamship Great Western.* 1963
Farr, Grahame.   *The Steamship Great Britain.* 1965

There are few good general historical treatments of Bristol. One of the best is:

Little, Bryan.   *The City and County of Bristol.* 1954, new ed 1967

Another recent and readable work, though slighter in content, is:

Ballard, C. M.   *Bristol, Sea-Port City.* 1966

An illustrated history of Bristol is being compiled in a series of booklets by Reece Winstone : *Bristol as it was.* Working backwards from *Bristol To-day* to 1860, there are at present nine volumes in this series, which provides the historian of Bristol with a remarkable collection of pictorial data.

Amongst basic texts for the student of Bristol history, the chronologies of J. Latimer are invaluable:

Annals of Bristol in the Nineteenth Century. Bristol, 1887
Annals of Bristol in the Eighteenth Century. Bristol, 1893

Although these volumes have long been out of print, they contain a mass of useful information culled largely from a careful reading of the local newspapers. Other well-established books are:

Arrowsmith, J. W.   *Dictionary of Bristol.* Bristol, 1st ed 1884, 2nd ed 1906
Stone, G. F.   *Bristol as it was—and as it is.* Bristol, 1909
Hutton, S.   *Bristol and its Famous Associations.* Bristol, 1907

The only general survey of port development is still:

Wells, C.   *A Short History of the Port of Bristol.* Bristol, 1909

On the industrial district to the east of Bristol, there are two useful books:

Ellacombe, H. T.   *The History of the Parish of Bitton.* Exeter, 1881
Braine, A.   *The History of Kingswood Forest.* Bristol, 1891, reprinted Bath, 1969

For the district to the south of Bristol, there are two more recent studies which touch on industrial aspects:

Atthill, R.   *Old Mendip.* Newton Abbot, 1964
Coysh, A. J., Mason, E. J., and Waite, V.   *The Mendips.* 1954

Some other modern works containing useful references on aspects of the industrial history of Bristol are:

Pevsner, N.   *The Buildings of Britain—North Somerset and Bristol.* 1958
Ison, W.   *The Georgian Buildings of Bristol.* 1952
MacInnes, C. M., and Whittard, W. F. (eds).   *Bristol and its adjoining Counties.* British Association, Bristol,
MacInnes, C. M.   *Bristol : A Gateway of Empire.* 2nd ed, Newton Abbot, 1968   /1955

Each industry and service has produced its own crop of literature, which cannot be adequately summarised here. For full bibliographical details, the reader should refer to the companion volume to the present work, *Industrial Archaeology of the Bristol Region,* pp 301-306.

For current research on industrial history and industrial archaeology in Bristol, the reader will find the publications of the Bristol Industrial Archaeological Society useful. These include a quarterly *Bulletin* and an annual *BIAS Journal.* Particulars may be obtained from The Secretary, BIAS, The City Museum, Queens Road, Bristol BS8 1RL.

ACKNOWLEDGMENTS

We are profoundly grateful to Mr Alan Warhurst, Director of Bristol City Museum, Mr Arnold Wilson, Director of Bristol City Art Gallery, and the Cultural Committee of Bristol Corporation, for permission to reproduce photographs and pictures from the Museum and Art Gallery collections. Many early photographs of the industrial and transport history of Bristol from the museum's archives are published here for the first time, and they provide a historical perspective without which this book would be the poorer. In addition, watercolours and pencil sketches from the remarkable Braikenridge Collection in the City Art Gallery have been useful in documenting the period of the early nineteenth century.

The following plates come from photographs in Bristol City Museum:

6, 7, 8, 9, 10, 11, 12, 13, 18A, 18B, 19A, 19B, 20, 21, 22, 23, 24B, 28, 29A, 29B, 31A, 31B, 32A, 33B, 35B, 37B, 38A, 39A, 40B, 42A, 42B, 44A, 44B, 48A, 49A, 55A, 55B, 56A, 60B, 70B, 72A, 72B, 73A, 73B, 74A, 74B, 76A, 76B, 77A, 77B, 78B, 79, 85A, 86A, 86B, 87A, 87B, 90A, 90B, 93, 94A, 94B, 95A, 95B, 96A, 96B, 97, 98B

The following plates come from pictures or sketches in Bristol City Art Gallery:

The frontispiece and dust cover illustration, 17, 32B, 37A, 69A, 78A, 88, 91B, 92A, 92B

The following plates are from photographs taken by Neil Cossons, the negatives of which now form part of the museum's collection:

16, 24A, 25A, 25B, 27, 30A, 41A, 47, 50B, 51A, 51B, 52A, 52B, 53B, 57A, 59, 61A, 61B, 62A, 62B, 63, 67, 68A, 69B, 75A, 75B, 80A, 80B, 81A, 99, 101, 103B, 104A, 104B, 105B

The following plates are from photographs by R. A. Buchanan:

54A, 54B, 68B, 89, 98A, 105A

We are very grateful to the following persons and organisations for permission to use their photographs, as indicated:

Aerofilms Ltd (14, 15, 33A, 36A, 71)
Mr S. T. Allen (46)
Mr C. H. T. Ashford (60A)
Mr Charles F. Cole (for E. N. Underwood & Partners) (65)
Bristol Commercial Vehicles Ltd (83B, 84B)
Bristol Evening Post (35A)
British Aircraft Corporation (Filton Division) (85B)
J. S. Fry & Sons (Cadbury Brothers Ltd) (56B)
The Great Britain Steamship Preservation Project (43B)
Mr S. H. P. Higgins (82A, 82B, 83A, 84A)
Mr John Hucklebridge (57B)
Illustrated London News (London Electrotype Agency) (49B, 103A)
The National Maritime Museum, Greenwich (43A)
Messrs R. Pearse and J. Cornwell (50A)
The Port of Bristol Authority (30B, 34A, 34B, 40A, 41A, 45, 66, 91A, 100, 107)
H. & T. Proctor Ltd (53A)
E. S. & A. Robinson (Holdings) Ltd (58A, 58B, 64)
Mr John C. Sawtell (70A)
The late Mr Fred Sharp (26, 39B, 41B)
Stothert & Pitt Ltd (38B)
The Times (106)
Mr George Watkins (48B)

INDEX